For all who
live in the
animal world

First published by Allen & Unwin in 2025

Allen & Unwin
Cammeraygal Country
83 Alexander Street
Crows Nest NSW 2065
Australia
Phone: (61 2) 8425 0100
Email: info@allenandunwin.com
Web: www.allenandunwin.com

Allen & Unwin acknowledges the Traditional Owners of the Country on which we live and work. We pay our respects to all Aboriginal and Torres Strait Islander Elders, past and present.

EU Authorised Representative: Easy Access System Europe, Mustamäe tee 50, 10621 Tallinn, Estonia, gpsr.requests@easproject.com

A catalogue record for this book is available from the National Library of Australia

ISBN 978 1 76118 156 6

For teaching resources, explore allenandunwin.com/learn

The illustrations were created using pen, watercolour and acrylics on Rains watercolour paper. Much of my inspiration comes from the natural beauty of the landscapes surrounding my hometown of Kuranda, as well as the lush scenery across the Atherton Tablelands. The colours, textures and forms found in these environments often guide the mood and detail of my illustrations. – Sandra Steffensen

Cover and text design by Sandra Nobes
Set in 26 pt Neuzeit SLT Std by Sandra Nobes
This book was printed in December 2025 in China by 1010 Printing Limited

3 5 7 9 10 8 6 4 2

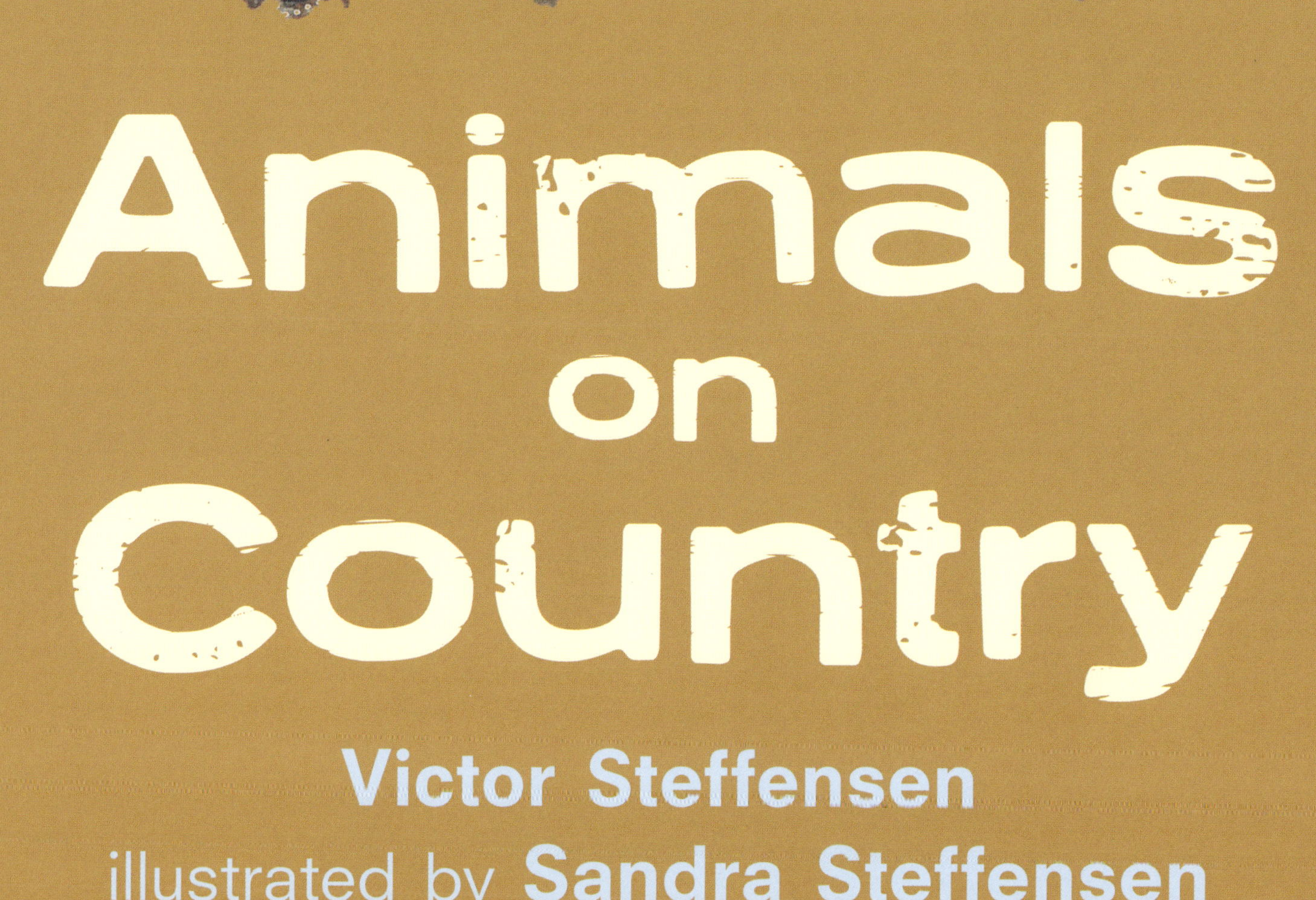

Animals on Country

Victor Steffensen
illustrated by **Sandra Steffensen**

ALLEN&UNWIN
SYDNEY • MELBOURNE • AUCKLAND • LONDON

Uncle Kuu is taking us for a walk in the bush to learn about animals. We need to walk **softly** and be very **quiet** if we are going to find them.

If you look carefully, you can see **fresh tracks** on the ground where different animals have been roaming around.

Uncle Kuu shows us **kangaroo** tracks, **dingo** tracks and even where an **emu** came walking past early this morning.

Uncle Kuu takes us to the riverside to meet his **totem** animal, the water goanna. He must care for the water goannas and cannot harm them or disturb the places where they live.

This special relationship between Aboriginal people and their totem animal means that every living thing has a chance to **survive**.

For thousands of years, Aboriginal people looked after the land to keep it **healthy**, so there was plenty of food for the animals to eat.

They took good care of the **trees** so that certain animals like possums could make a home in their hollow branches.

They took care of the **rivers** and **oceans** so there would be plenty of **fish** swimming around for everyone to see.

Making sure the waters were kept **clean** gave all the animals, **big** and **small**, a healthy place to live.

Uncle Kuu tells us about **story places** – special areas where the animals could **roam free** and **breed** lots of babies into the world. In these places, Aboriginal people were not allowed to hunt or disturb the Country in any way.

Some animals eat other animals for food, which is all part of the natural food chain created by **Mother Nature**.

Aboriginal people ate many different animals that were not their totems, but would only take **enough** to feed themselves. Taking too much is being **greedy** and will mean there are fewer animals to catch next time.

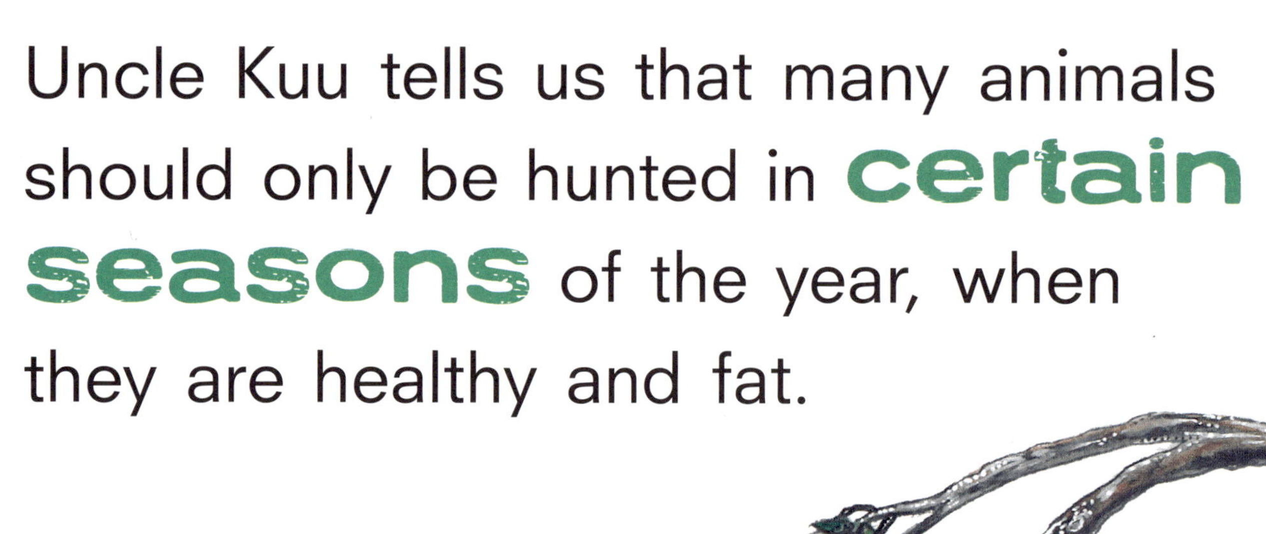

Uncle Kuu tells us that many animals should only be hunted in **certain seasons** of the year, when they are healthy and fat.

Like when the golden wattle tree shoots its yellow flowers, it is the right time to catch a nice big fish to **share** with the family.

Uncle Kuu says if you eat an animal, it is important to be respectful and thankful to the animal's **spirit**, and to the Country where the animal comes from.

Aboriginal people followed the lores of **caring for Country** for so long that the animals depended on them to look after the land and waters. They made **songs** and **dances** about the animals, so the knowledge would never be lost.

Today, the animals are wondering what has happened to the people. Trees have been **cut down** and land has been **cleared**. Too many animals have been hunted or fished in the **wrong season**, until there are only a few left to catch.

Uncle Kuu says if there are not many animals, then we must not hunt at all to give them and the Country a **rest** for a while, until they are plentiful again.

Uncle Kuu takes us to the river and shows us a place where lots of **pollution** is running into the water from a nearby factory. There used to be lots of fish, turtles and platypuses living here, but they are now gone because the water is **poisonous**.

Uncle Kuu says that the animals miss the way Aboriginal people have **helped** the land with **cool fires**. Today, big bushfires are threatening the lives and homes of all the animals and it is because the people don't look after the Country with fire anymore.

People need to start **caring** for the animals again and **protecting** their beautiful natural homes, so the animals have a **safe place** to live. Uncle Kuu gives each of us our very own **animal totem**, so that we can look after that animal for the rest of our lives.

All creatures, **big** and **small**,
will be so happy to see the people
caring for the animals once again
and to know that we are all part of the
animal world.

Uncle Kuu teaches us a new song about animals for us to **sing together** as we begin our walk all the way home.

(Chorus)
Aye – oh, let's take care of, the animals, the animals,
Aye – oh, let's take care of, the animals, the animals,

(Verse)
Take care of the water, for the fish in the sea,
Take care of the trees, for the birds and the bees,
Take care of the fire, so no one gets burnt,
Take care of the land, for the ones with feathers and fur,

(Chorus)
Aye – oh, let's take care of, the animals, the animals,
Aye – oh, let's take care of, the animals, the animals,

(Instrumental)

(Bridge)
We all live in the animal world,
Tell it to all the boys and girls,
We share Country with them each and every day,
And we live together in the most peculiar way,

(Chorus)

Aye – oh, let's take care of, the animals, the animals,
Aye – oh, let's take care of, the animals, the animals,
The animals, the animals, the animals, the animals.

The Animals

By Mulong

Scan this code to watch the video on YouTube